Coincidences,

Repeating Numbers, & More

Signs From The Universe

How To Recognize & Interpret

These Life-Changing Messages

By

Kelly Wallace

Professional Psychic Counselor

<u>DrKellyPsychic.com</u>[1]

Table of Contents

Books by Kelly Wallace

———

10 Minutes A Day to A Powerful New Life

Become Your Higher Self – Using Spiritual Energy to Transform Your Life

Breaking The Worry Habit – Stop Your Anxious Thoughts And Start Living!

Chakras – Heal, Clear, And Strengthen Your Energy Centers

Clear Your Karma – The Healing Power of Your Past Lives

Contacting Your Spirit Guides – Meeting and Working with Your Invisible Helpers

Creating A Charmed Life – Enchantments to Attract, Repel, Cleanse & Heal

Dream Work – Using The Wisdom Of Your Sleeping Mind To Change Your Waking Life

Energy Work – Heal, Cleanse, and Strengthen Your Aura

Everyday Miracles – Powerful Steps to Wonderful Experiences

Finding Your Life Purpose – Uncover Your Soul's True Goals

Healing the Child Within – Rewrite Your Early Childhood Life Script

About Kelly Wallace

Kelly is a bestselling spiritual and self-help author, former radio show host, and has been a professional psychic counselor for over twenty years. She can see, hear, sense, and feel information sent from Spirit, the Universe, and a client's Higher Self.

She offers professional psychic counseling, caring guidance, and solutions that work! More than just a typical psychic reading or counseling session, you will feel you've found a real friend during your time of need—whether you simply want answers and guidance to your current worries or concerns, or you're interested in learning more about your soulmate, spirit guides, angels, past lives, or anything else.

Contact her today for an in-depth and life-altering reading!

Website: DrKellyPsychic.com[1]

Email: Dr.Kelly.Psychic.Counselor@gmail.com

---

1. http://psychicreadingsbydrkelly.webs.com/

What This Book Covers

You Are Never Alone

———

Whether you're trying to find answers to questions in your life, solutions to problems, or higher guidance, the Universe can help. In fact, the Universe is always talking, we just need to learn to listen and understand the messages then take action on them.

The reason it's so hard to interpret all of this wisdom that's right in front of you is because the Universe has a language of its own. Once you learn what these signs mean for you personally your life will expand in both subtle and wondrous ways. It's comforting to know that no matter what you're going through in life you're never alone.

Where These Messages Come From

First, let me cover what I believe the "Universe" is. Some feel that the Universe is a collective consciousness of all the wisdom we humans have now and have ever had. Since everything and everyone is made of energy, it all gathers into the Universe and that knowledge is available to anyone who knows how to tap into it.

Others feel that wisdom from the Universe is simply your own soul, your higher self. You've lived many lives and all of the lessons you've learned and the wisdom you've gathered is right there inside of you.

And some feel that these messages of higher guidance come from angels, spirit guides, and/or deceased relatives. In fact, my grandmother often steps in to help me!

For myself, I believe in each one. Why not? They're all very likely and I'll take positive guidance from whatever source it is. Also, through my own meditations and doing psychic readings for so long, I can tell where each message comes from. Every source has its own unique energy vibration and type of guidance.

I think of it this way, it's like talking to the various people you know in life and getting input from them. Each person has their own voice and experiences, right? When they offer you advice it's unique to the person. So, too, is the advice we get from the "Universe". For the sake of simplicity, I'll be referring to this wisdom as coming from the Universe. Although, as you become more comfortable with it you might find that the guidance sent to you comes from one or more sources.

Getting Started

———

Very soon you'll start receiving messages easily and frequently. It will be effortless and help from higher up will flow smoothly into your life. Getting into the right mindset is important to noticing and being able to use this guidance though.

Be Open To Receiving

It seems obvious that if you're seeking help from the Universe that you're open to its guidance, but nearly everyone holds some worry or doubt. Although we want answers we're also uneasy about what the messages might be. What if it's something you don't want to hear or is too difficult to follow?

We also wonder if what we receive truly is special information for us, or just wishful—or fearful—thinking. This apprehension gets in the way of receiving helpful messages. It's a block between you and the Universal energy that's sending the assistance you need. However, just because you're uncertain or wary doesn't mean you won't get the help you're looking for, it just means you'll have to pay closer attention.

Then again, if you aren't ready to receive these answers then you won't. When friends or clients tell me they haven't gotten any helpful answers, I tell them it's because they aren't ready to receive them yet.

We need to be ready and willing to change for us to process the fact that we're receiving higher guidance. If you aren't ready you simply won't see it or if you do it won't make any sense or lead anywhere. As time goes on and you become comfortable with receiving these messages you'll find that you relax more into it and are far more open to this assistance.

Just having a true desire to hear from the Universe and the guidance it can offer is enough to get you started. Remind yourself that you're prepared to accept the answers sent your way, no matter what they are or where they come from—as long as it's positive.

Messages from the Universe present themselves in so many ways. I'll talk about that more in-depth in a moment, but keep in mind that signs can come from things as random as a complete stranger or the cover of a book and everything in between. This is why it's so important to learn how to be open to the messages and then learning to interpret them.

Pay Attention

When you ask the Universe for guidance be sure you're also paying attention to any coincidences, patterns, or other ways it might be trying to communicate with you. One time I had been wondering if I should start a certain business. I felt it could be a good idea, but it would involve a lot of work and time, so I had put it off for a long while. I asked the Universe to send me some guidance and, sure enough, it arrived that very afternoon.

A friend of mine came over to visit and he was wearing a T-shirt. That might not seem like anything out of the ordinary, but I had never seen him wear a T-shirt the entire time I'd known him. He always preferred button-up shirts. Also, it was a Nike T-shirt with "Just Do It" printed on it. I smiled to myself and knew the Universe was telling me it was time to finally dive in and start this business. In other words, just do it instead of thinking about it.

The intelligence of the Universe is infinite, is always connected to you, and always finding ways to help you. Although, we don't always realize this, especially when we're going through stressful times. When life is difficult we tend to turn inward and focus on our current problems, which is why we often miss those subtle, or not so subtle, messages from higher up. By paying more attention to your environment and the things you're experiencing you'll probably be surprised at how much guidance actually comes your way.

Take Notes

I have a small journal I keep with me at all times to record any signs or messages I receive. At the top of a blank page I'll write down the date and my current question, problem, or goal, then leave it in the hands of the Universe. I then keep my mind, eyes, and ears open for any guidance that comes my way.

How will you know if something is important enough to write down? It just feels different, and once you become more familiar with receiving signs from the Universe and interpreting them you'll know exactly what I'm talking about.

In fact, I bet you've already experienced a few or even several times when information was sent to you. It's those things that pop up out of nowhere and make you take notice. Something out of the ordinary or something that strikes a chord and you know the experience was significant.

I also keep notes of recurring experiences such as songs that keep showing up, symbols or logos or words, anything that comes into my life repeatedly, especially when I'm seeking answers. I then make a note of them in my journal. You don't have to do this, but it's helpful to see what information has come your way since it's easy to forget.

Never discard patterns or coincidences thinking they're nothing. These repeats show up for a reason. We don't always get it at first though, so writing it down is extremely helpful. More often than not, the Universe will keep sending the message again and again, either in exactly the same way or a different form but with a similar meaning, until we finally get it.

Take Action

When you do receive guidance and the opportunity arises, make sure you take advantage of it. Second-guessing yourself, being uncertain of the message(s) you received, and waiting until you're "really, really sure" will create obstacles or halt progress completely. Like that T-shirt my friend was wearing, sometimes you've got to "Just Do It".

One time my son-in-law had lost his job due to major cutbacks in the company. He wasn't having luck finding anything new and was getting pretty stressed about it. In between looking for work he started going back to school part-time, hoping to finally finish his bachelor's degree. While on campus he had seen one particular teacher that really stuck out since he was well over six-feet tall with long, snow-white hair, and always had a bright green backpack slung over one shoulder.

It wasn't anything special seeing him around the college area, but one day my son-in-law was at a record shop nearly an hour away from the school and this teacher happened to be there! In the background the song *Money, That's What I Want*, by Barrett Strong was playing. My son-in-law took it as a clear message and went over to say hello to the teacher. (He took action!) They started talking and discussed their love of music. As the conversation progressed the teacher offered him an internship that paid decently and would look great on his resume.

This might just seem like good luck, but my son-in-law is notoriously introverted and would never just walk up to someone and strike up a conversation. However, he knew that seeing this teacher had to be something important, not to mention the very fitting song playing at the record store. He was open to receiving guidance from the Universe and grabbed the chance when it came along.

Signs Should Resonate

Since we're all connected to the Universe and vice versa it's going to send you messages that resonate. You'll know the information is specifically meant for you because you'll feel it on some level. Even if you don't understand it, your higher self is going to alert you to the fact that there's something important about the person, occurrence, symbol, song, or pattern. Once you start recognizing and following the guidance sent to you, more doors will open and life will become easier.

Keep in mind though that once you do start becoming more aware of these messages from higher up you could get into the habit of seeing what you want to see. That's why it's important to pay attention to yourself to see if this really resonates in your gut or just in your mind.

I've too often seen friends and clients who wanted the Universe to tell them something specific so they would bend or twist any supposed sign that came their way as proof that they should or shouldn't do something. When you get true messages that are meant to help you it's effortless and fills you with a sense of knowing. You just know it's important somehow and don't have to force it.

Recently, a friend of mine wanted to go on vacation to Mexico, even though Covid was still running rampant in the US and all over the world, and with no vaccine as yet. Needless to say, it was a bad idea. However, she wouldn't be deterred. She asked the Universe if she should go, and right away she started getting "signs that it was okay".

In reality, she was seeing what she wanted to see. If she had been honest with herself she would have noticed that the things she claimed were messages from the Universe telling her to go was just her own wishful thinking.

She and her husband ended up going, even though her doctor told her what a bad idea it was. They stayed for a week, had a great time, got back to the US, and less than a week later both she and her husband were in the hospital due to complications related to Covid. She was released a week later but her husband had to be put into a medically induced coma for three days and was on a ventilator. Thankfully, he recovered.

This story isn't meant to scare you, just to be very aware of how you feel when you receive guidance from the Universe. It's so important to be absolutely honest with yourself about the information you see or hear. Also, what do the people who care about you think as well? Sure, sometimes we need to take calculated risks, but we shouldn't be foolish just because we want something so badly.

The way to avoid your ego getting involved is to be sure you've released your personal expectations about your goal. Just allow the guidance to come when and how it's meant to. Remind yourself that if you're seeking help it's because you don't have the answers. If you already have the answer or know what you want to do, then waiting for signs doesn't often work because you'll interpret it to fit your expectations.

Keep It Simple

It's exciting when you start noticing the Universe showing up here and there to help you along in life. You receive a sign, a coincidence, or see a symbol that feels very important and right away you want to make sense of it. This is the easiest way to overcomplicate things and get yourself lost and more confused when your real goal is to seek the truth.

The Universe tends to be pretty simple and straightforward with its guidance, we just need to learn to interpret it without thinking too long and hard about the information. I can't count how many times I've gotten a recurring symbol, heard a recurring word, or some other pattern and I tried unraveling the mystery of it as if I was Sherlock Holmes. I thought to myself, "What could that mean?" Then I'd come up with ten different possibilities that could make perfect sense though I'd just get myself more confused and felt more uncertain.

In the end, the answer was always plain as day and so easy. Sure, many times hindsight is 20/20 and that's okay. It's often easier to make sense of something after it's already happened. Then we find ourselves saying, "Oh, that was so simple! Why didn't I get that?"

Being human, it's common for us to get in our own way and cloud our thinking. This is especially true when it comes to receiving and interpreting answers from the Universe. There's no need to dig any deeper or follow the clues to the ends of the earth.

One summer day I wasted an entire afternoon at a huge antique store simply because the sign out front called to me. I felt for certain that there was a bigger clue and more guidance to be found inside. No, the Universe just wanted me to see this shop name and use that as guidance, not pick through everything inside the store.

Now I know when I receive signs I pay attention and, yes, I do think about it, but I don't try to take it any further. I know that when the time is right everything will come together. I remind myself that in that brief moment is when the Universe is talking to me, it's not trying to have a full-blown conversation. When a sign impacts me I know it's special in that very moment and I'll be led in the right direction if I remain aware and stay out of my own way.

No matter how badly you want to know something, remind yourself that when you truly need to know or are ready to know, the Universe will contact you. A sign or message will arrive and you'll know what problem or goal it pertains to. You might not know exactly what the message is telling you, so try not to read too much into it. Just let things play out. Signs aren't meant to be tricky, like some mystery that needs to be solved. The Universe is always here to help us, so let it help, and pay attention to what it's telling you.

The Universe Is Your Copilot

Although life can seem overwhelming at times, believing in higher guidance releases some of the pressure. Knowing that there's something bigger and wiser helping to guide you, understanding the reasons why things are happening *for* you—not to you—helps to shift your perspective. When you make that shift you'll start seeing your life and the entire world differently. Many times it's not that things change, it's that you change, and that's when life truly starts getting better.

One important lesson we need to learn is that *we* are the creators of our own lives. Yes, outside influences can affect us, but we have much more control over our destinies than we sometimes believe we do. You aren't put on this earth for one predestined path and that's that. You have choices, many of them.

The Universe works with us as a co-creator, our copilot. It's not going to step in and dictate where you go. Instead, it will help to point you in the right direction if you get lost, give you a push if you're stagnant, and get your attention if you're distracted. When we receive these messages it's up to us to take the information or opportunity and *make* things happen.

Asking For Signs

―――――

My grandmother used to tell me, "If you don't speak up nobody will hear you." This is the same with the Universe. Although it can and does send you guidance without you even saying a word, sometimes just asking for help or inspiration works the best and fastest. It shows the Universe that you're open to receiving messages of guidance and are keeping an eye out for anything that comes your way.

I know this seems too simple to work, but sometimes all you need to do is ask and you'll get it. Whether you want help from a friend or help from the Universe, this works more often than not. So why don't we do it? Maybe it's stubborn pride that keeps us from reaching out. Or perhaps we somehow feel weak by asking for help or worry that we'll be rejected. That's usually not the case though with friends and family, and it's never the case where the Universe is concerned.

Where To Start

The easiest thing to do is ask for a sign that you'll recognize. This could be a symbol, a person, a number, whatever is important to you, but make sure you give the Universe room to work. I wouldn't ask for something very specific such as, "If I'm meant to be in a long-term relationship with this current person I'm dating then give me a sign by having him talk about marriage."

What I usually do is say something like, "If it's for my highest good to take this opportunity (a person, job, move, whatever it might be) please send me a recurring symbol or important song lyrics." For myself, these mean the most. Some people prefer dream messages, numbers, or personalized license plates. Yes, I have a friend who narrowed down how he prefers receiving guidance to messages on license plates. It works for him but isn't something I would notice much.

Choose what works for you. Or, better yet, ask for a sign but allow the Universe to choose what it sends to you. The easiest thing to request is a repeating symbol and let the Universe choose what this will be. Very often the symbol itself will have meaning or will eventually lead to the answer you're seeking.

Don't give up if you don't see anything immediately. Just let the Universe know you're open to receiving your sign and you eventually will. When I put in a specific request that I knew I wouldn't miss, it took weeks before I saw the sign I asked for, but it came exactly when I needed it most.

Using Oracle Cards

———

Whether tarot cards, angel cards, or other oracle cards, any of these will work to receive guidance from the Universe. I prefer using tarot cards since they're so rich in color and symbolism. Regardless of which you use, the simplest way to use them is to shuffle the deck, ask your question, and lay down one card. Upright would be a "yes" answer and reversed would be "no".

You might be thinking, "Isn't this just random?" Or, "Why would I leave the fate of my life in the hands of a deck of cards?" I've used tarot and other oracle cards for decades now and have seen for myself that the Universe and our higher selves can easily come through in them.

More than just a yes or no answer, when you flip the card over after asking for guidance, how do you feel when you see the upright or reversed card? Let's say that you asked whether you should start looking for a new job and the card came up reversed. So, the answer would be no.

Think about how this answer feels to you. Do you feel relieved? Disappointed? Nervous? Worried? Angry? Happy? If you tune into yourself you should feel some sort of reaction bubbling up.

Let's say that you asked about whether or not you should take a new job offer, the card was reversed (no), and you feel disappointed. Now, go in deeper. Why are you disappointed? Have you wanted out of your current job for some time? Or, do you feel relieved because, even if you believe you should find another job, you're well-established in your current position? Though in a way that disappoints you because you have a tendency to not take calculated risks in life?

Truth be told, there are probably good reasons to stay or go. And you know what? You don't have to take the advice the cards offer. You can do the exact opposite. Maybe you'll look back on it and think the cards were right all along and the Universe was guiding you or warning you. Or, maybe the cards were completely wrong. Perhaps the Universe wanted to get you out of your comfort zone and, by giving a contrary answer to what you truly wanted, it propelled you to finally take action.

If you want more information on reading oracle cards I go into detail in my book *Intuitive Tarot – Learn To Read The Tarot Instantly.* But it really is as simple as keeping your question or situation in mind, then taking a look at the random card you pulled. What emotion does it evoke? Does the figure in the card, any symbols, or colors seem to offer direction?

I'll never forget this time when I was going on a job interview. I had asked the Universe whether I should keep trying to make my at-home businesses work or get a "real job" with a steady paycheck. I got my tarot cards, shuffled them, and pulled a card out at random. It was the Emperor reversed. The easiest answer would be "no".

However, I set the bar a little higher and didn't really ask a yes or no question. I wanted actual guidance. As I looked at the card I noticed the man in the card was reversed. To me, this meant that the interview I was going on could be with a male and he might not be as positive as I would hope for.

I also noticed that the Emperor was wearing a green robe and green is usually associated with healing and money. So, perhaps this job would make me feel bad mentally or emotionally, and in the long run, the money wouldn't outweigh the stress. I also took note that the card was the number 4. In my mind, being reversed would be "less than four". But I needed to see how that would play out.

Not wanting to put my life in the hands of a single tarot card I went on the job interview. Sure enough, the person who interviewed me was a man and he had a very off-putting personality. He was too laid back yet seemed to act like he ran the place and, with a snap of his finger, people would do his bidding. In other words, he had a big ego and that rubbed me the wrong way. I also found that, even with all my prior experience, I would start out with lower pay until I proved myself. To top it all off, it was supposed to be a 5 day/40-hour a week job, but in reality, it was three days and only 15 hours per week.

Needless to say, I politely declined the position and was very relieved I did. It also amazed me (and still does to this day) how accurate the cards are when we're open to the guidance the Universe sends through them.

One thing I want to stress is that oracle cards aren't predicting your future and telling you what to do. It's just a conduit for the Universe to come through and help you. In the end, you're the one who gets to make the decisions and very often the cards tap into what you already know or suspect. In turn, they bring it to the surface for you to become more aware and make the best decision for yourself and your life.

Knowing that the Universe can communicate with you in different ways helps to lift the pressure of tough decisions and confusion. Life is easier when you realize you aren't on your own, just thrown into a world and groping around. The Universe is always by your side, giving you signs, and working for your highest good.

How The Universe Communicates

———

Now I want to get into the many ways the Universe tries to communicate with you. As you'll see, there are a lot! Don't let it all overwhelm you though. At first, it will seem like messages can come from anywhere and everywhere—and they can.

This is what's so wonderful about the Universe though. Since everything is made of energy, the Universe can easily come through in any of the following ways to help you. With time and attention, you'll notice which of these are strongest for you and it will soon feel completely natural. Eventually, receiving this type of guidance will be part of your everyday life.

1. Numbers

Repeating Numbers -

Also known as angel numbers, these are a series of repeating numbers and are the easiest to spot. You look at the clock and the time is 11:11, 1:11, 2:22, 3:33, or so on. The next day it happens again. Or, you drive by a house and notice the address has a repeating number and you see the number again, and again.

The more times a number is repeated, the stronger the message. For example, seeing 11:11 repeatedly is a much stronger message than if you see 1:11 or just 11. However, they all have importance. Also, you can tell if something is going to increase or decrease depending on the amount of numbers you see.

For example, there was a time when I was going through a really rough patch in life. I would look at the clock and see the time of 11:11 again and again. Rather than taking it as any specific message, I felt comforted knowing the Universe was watching over me and that "this too shall pass".

Then a few weeks later I would randomly look at the clock and notice that it was 1:11. One less number. And guess what? My situation had gotten a little better by that time. Soon I stopped seeing the repeating numbers altogether and my problem was behind me as well.

On the other hand, if I see the number increasing, say from 1:11 to 11:11, I know that the energy will become stronger. It doesn't mean something bad will happen, it's just the Universe telling you to wake up and pay attention.

An increase in numbers can be telling you that something could potentially get worse so take care of it now rather than later. Or, that the energies for a positive opportunity are increasing so be sure to take advantage of it before it passes.

Random Numbers -

You can also see random numbers that mean something special to you. It could be an important day like a birthday or anniversary, or your favorite number. I see birth dates the most and if they repeat more than two or three times I know it pertains to that person somehow.

I often see 12:23, which was my mother's birth date, when the anniversary of her death approaches. To me, it's a reassuring sign letting me know that she's okay and to remember her life rather than her passing.

Earlier this year I started seeing 10:15 a lot on the clock. This is my fourth daughter's birthday, so I knew the sign had something to do with her. She works for a health clinic and a few weeks after receiving this sign repeatedly she called to tell me she had Covid. She was very sick for two weeks but made a full recovery. The sign I kept receiving wasn't a warning, something meant to scare me. Instead, it was a message of comfort that she would be okay.

I'm not going to get into the subject of numerology here only because, as I mentioned previously, it's better to just pay attention and acknowledge the sign rather than trying to think too hard about what it could mean.

One thing is for certain though, any sign from the Universe, especially when it repeats, is a clear message that something important is coming up—whether an opportunity, a change, or a person. Sometimes, it's just a message of comfort.

2. Boredom, Anxiety, Discontent

None of those emotions sound positive and that's precisely why these are signs from the Universe. In fact, any recurring negative emotion is a huge indicator that something needs to change in your life.

If you feel uncomfortable long enough or your discomfort is intense you're going to do something about it. If not, you'll just keep doing the same things or ignoring the situation yet expecting life to change without your help. The longer you ignore it, the louder the message will become until you finally take action or things eventually fall apart and you're forced to do something about it.

3. Through People

I'm not sure how this happens, but the Universe can use people as vehicles to relay messages to you. I honestly don't feel the person is "possessed" for those moments, but they could feel compelled to do or say something that gets your attention.

It's like, on a subconscious level, the Universe asks them to relay a message and they gladly do so without realizing just how important it is for you. Afterward, you'll probably think to yourself or tell someone, "That was just too weird not to be a sign!"

- Direct Contact

You get a text or phone call or could meet a random person who gives you valuable information exactly when you need it.

Years ago, I was about to buy a house with my then-husband. Our marriage had been rocky for a while, but I assumed we would work through it and everything would be okay. We had gone to look at a house the day before and were set on getting it. One of the things I asked the Universe was whether or not buying a house with him was such a good idea. Okay, simply *asking* that question alone should have been a strong clue, right? So often we ignore our intuition though, no matter how loud it's screaming at us.

Anyway, I was at the store doing grocery shopping and thinking about our soon-to-be home. Out of nowhere, a man walked up to me, looked me in the eyes, and said, "Don't sign the papers." He then walked away. I didn't need any more guidance on that issue, I had my answer! I didn't sign the papers, we didn't get the house, and we were soon divorced afterward. Had I not asked for higher guidance or if I had ignored what that stranger said to me, it would have been a mess with owning a home together.

- Indirect Contact

It might seem rude to eavesdrop on a conversation between two strangers, but sometimes the Universe wants us to hear it because the information is helpful to us personally.

I was at the mall one evening with a close friend of mine having dinner in the food court. She had gotten out of a long-term relationship several months earlier, felt she had healed from it, and was ready to find love again but was nervous about putting herself out there. As I was listening to her, I noticed two women at the table next to us talking about the very same thing. Coincidence? Yes! And so I told my friend to pay attention as we quietly ate.

The other two ladies weren't whispering so it was easy to hear them. One said she wanted to be in love again but wasn't brave enough to go the online dating route. Her friend was the opposite and was excitedly talking about the wonderful new man she just met on a certain dating site. She said she did have to weed through people who didn't seem to be a good match, but loved that she got to know each person a little bit before ever leaving her house. She and this man were about to go on their third date and things seemed really positive.

My friend just looked at me and smiled. I told her, "You see, there's a part of you that's afraid to try dating again and prefers being single and the other part of you that wants to take a risk and find love again. Judging by the signs—" I glanced at the women near us then back at my friend. "It seems like the part of you that wants to take a risk and try online dating will probably be rewarded." She did and she was.

That's not to say that every overheard conversation is important or that we should invade others' privacy. As you get used to picking up on signs from the Universe you'll know what's useful and what isn't.

4. Synchronicity

These are events that happen out of nowhere yet get your attention. Those seemingly random occurrences that feel lucky or coincidental though are somehow related.

For example, let's say you've wanted to move but you weren't sure where. You're out one day and see someone carrying a bouquet of brightly colored flowers, then you get to work and notice a coworker has a bouquet of flowers on their desk. On your drive home the road you usually take is closed off due to repairs and you take a detour. As you go on this other street you notice a house with brightly colored flowers in the front and it just happens to be for sale or rent. This isn't a mere coincidence!

Synchronicity is one of the most powerful ways the Universe communicates with us. The more you're awake and aware of its guidance the more you'll start experiencing them. And, something nice about synchronicity is most of the time you don't have to read deeply into it. You don't need to decipher the clues or use intuition to figure out what it means. It's as simple as recognizing that the Universe is getting your attention, paying attention, then eventually an opportunity or answer will present itself. Once it does, all you need to do is follow it.

Synchronicities are a direct message from the Universe letting you know you're on the right path.

5. Songs

Have you woken up with a song stuck in your head or a special-to-you song comes on the radio? Perhaps lyrics from a random song seem to leap out at you. You could also hear the same song, again and again, but at different times. Someone who passes by you could even be singing a certain song.

Pay attention to the specific lyrics that you hear since there could be a message in them for you. Just like my son-in-law knew the lyrics to the song, *Money, That's What I Want*, were important for him and led him to a well-paying internship.

If the song has meaning to you such as it bringing up a memory from a vacation, college, your wedding, or something else special, interpret the meaning of the sign from that perspective. Perhaps it's a reminder that you need a vacation, to contact and reconnect with a friend, or do something special with your spouse.

A friend of mine had thought about starting a business with her cousin. Although she felt eager and hopeful, they had very different personalities and goals. I told her before making a final decision to be open to any signs from the Universe and then see what happens.

That very evening she was watching TV and flipping through the channels. There was a song playing on a particular station and she stopped, wide-eyed. It was the Fleetwood Mac song, *Go Your Own Way*. Instantly, she knew it was a message for her saying she should do her own thing rather than a partnership with her cousin. She smiled and breathed a sigh of relief. All along she knew it was a bad idea, but until the Universe stepped in and offered her this sign she questioned herself.

6. Random Thoughts

Sometimes a thought can jump into your mind seemingly out of nowhere. Maybe it's an idea, a solution, or inspiration to do something. Or, it could be about a person. If this thought is helpful be sure you pay attention to it and what it means for your personal situation or goal.

I've had thoughts spring up wondering about friends or family—so I check in on them—or solutions that had me saying, "Hmm...why didn't I think of this sooner?"

7. Words or Pictures

You could see a billboard, a book or magazine, a road sign, a social media post, or something else and it feels like a special message for you. The picture or words resonate either consciously and you know exactly what it means, or at a deeper level yet you still know it's important and all will be revealed to you soon.

I had put off getting new glasses for far too long. My old glasses weren't working as well, but going to the eye doctor, choosing new frames, waiting for the glasses to come in, then getting used to the new prescription had me setting it aside. Well, the Universe finally stepped in and gave me the push I needed.

I was going to the store with one of my daughters and when we got out of the car I saw that someone had dropped their glasses and a car had obviously run over them. The message registered only slightly in my mind. On our way home I saw a new billboard and it was for an optometrist. Okay, the message was a little stronger this time, though I still probably wouldn't have taken action.

The Universe knew this as well because later that evening I took my glasses off to clean them. I was in the kitchen, dropped them, a lens popped out, my cat jumped on it thinking it was a toy and the lens ended up under the refrigerator within two seconds. Well, now I had no choice but to finally make an appointment to get new glasses!

Another example is, one of my daughters tends to be a workaholic. She doesn't need the extra money that comes with working overtime, but she has the determination to always be busy. As she was driving to work one day she saw a new sign close to her job that said, "Slow down, children at play." Looking to her right, she saw a small park that she had obviously driven by hundreds of times yet never noticed. Since all of my girls grew up with my same spiritual streak she took it as a sign for herself to slow down and take some time out to play, which she did.

There are so many different ways we can receive signs and interpreting them is different for everyone. Just follow your intuition and try not to overthink things too much. Messages are usually pretty clear. If not, they'll be clear to you very soon.

8. Dreams

The Universe, spirit guides, and loved ones who have crossed over can come through easily in our dreams. You can incubate the dream by asking a certain question or for guidance on something important, then fall asleep as usual. The following morning think about your dreams and if anything in them could be a message for you. Or, sometimes a dream will just stand out even if you didn't ask for help on anything.

So, how will you know if the dream was important?

- The dream was intense and felt very real.

- You met someone important to you.

- You were told something or shown something.

- You have a recurring dream. (Same theme, person, symbols, or place.)

- You have recurring nightmares. (This is probably something inside you that needs healing.)

- You dream about a certain time in your life. (Is there an issue that needs to be resolved?)

- You see a word or symbol in your dream then see this in real life very soon after.

I've gotten amazing help and guidance over the years through dream work. I've also healed old emotional wounds, reconnected with loved ones and beloved pets, gotten ideas and inspiration, and so much more. Anyone who believes that dreams are just subconscious nonsense is truly missing out.

9. Hearing Voices

This one can sometimes be a little shocking. You're just starting to drift off to sleep or are immersed in work or a task and you hear someone say your name or another word yet you're alone. The Universe does this to, obviously, get your attention.

Hearing your name means that you aren't paying full attention to the signs they've been sending so they want you to wake up and take notice. And what better way than to jar you out of near-sleep or intense concentration?

Sometimes I've heard words too. Once as I was starting to fall asleep I heard a man's voice in my ear saying, "Start over!" I knew right away what this was referring to. I had been working on a book and was really struggling with it. With all of my experience as a psychic and a writer I should have known that the subject or slant of the book just wasn't working out, but I tend to be stubborn—and waste a lot of time doing so. Well, when I got that message I smiled to myself and in the morning I scrapped what I had written and started over. The book went smoothly after that.

10. Odd Sensations

You know that feeling you get when you're completely alone though it's like static electricity fills the room? It feels as if someone is standing near you, or right in back of you, but you look and nothing is there. The hairs on the back of your neck might stand up or you could get goosebumps. This is the Universal energy tapping into you, trying to get your attention.

Usually, no message comes along with this, just the fact that you need to pay attention. It's like an invisible tap on the shoulder letting you know you aren't alone and that if you need guidance it will soon be making an appearance.

11. Feathers, Coins, Etc.

Whenever you keep encountering a certain item it's a sure sign that the Universe is trying to get your attention. In my own life, I often receive white feathers from my grandmother. It's her way of letting me know she's nearby and to be on the lookout for change or opportunity.

A client of mine finds silverware. How odd is that? But it's her own personal sign from the Universe and one she won't miss. After all, finding a metal spoon or fork on the ground somewhere isn't all that common. But when she does, she knows it's a special message for her.

A friend finds old pennies when the Universe is trying to speak to him, another encounters yellow sports cars, and another sees red shoes. Although feathers and coins are the most common way we're contacted, for many people they have their own unique symbol so the Universe knows they'll pay attention.

12. Intuition

This one is far too easy to ignore. We shrug off those gut feelings that tell us something seems "right" or "off". We doubt our intuition because, for some reason, we believe we need outside proof to be sure it's real. We shouldn't though. All energy is connected. Since the Universe holds energy (and is infinitely wise) and you do as well, it makes sense that you can intuitively tap into its messages for yourself.

If you're unsure about trusting that deep knowing inside of you I recommend getting a small notebook (I'm a firm believer in writing things down!) and make notes any time you have a strong feeling in your gut. See how it plays out then compare the reality of what happened with what your intuition said to you. More often than not you'll see that you're right.

This is especially helpful when you meet new people or want to pursue a new path in life. After meeting this person, tune into how you feel and write this down. Even if you only get a few words, emotions, or even symbols. Before taking on that new position at work, going on that first date, starting a business, or choosing a career or college major, focus on the sensations in your body and how you *truly* feel about it.

These feelings are your truth and your truth has a direct connection with the Universe. Once you start listening to this voice inside you it will become stronger over time and you'll feel more certain that you're making the right decisions. You'll also open yourself up to better people and better opportunities.

13. Technical Difficulties

If the internet goes out, your text won't go through, your computer freezes, your TV shuts off, or that movie you want to watch just won't load, it's a sign you might want to pay attention to. Of course, while these might mean absolutely nothing except an interruption in something you want to accomplish, sometimes there's good reason to look a bit deeper.

One time I was feeling irritated about something my boyfriend had said. I believed he was insensitive and I felt hurt. Instead of being honest with him about my feelings, I had started writing an angry text that would "hurt him as much as he hurt me". (Immature, I know!) I went to hit the send button and right before that my phone shut off. When I rebooted it, the text was gone. I'll admit, I was relieved. I took it as a message from the Universe to think before I act and react. I'm much more careful now.

If this happens to you, take a moment to think about what you're saying in the text or email. If it didn't send the first time, do you really want to try again? Maybe you need to rephrase what you're saying, or not send it at all. In other words, the Universe is giving you a second chance so be sure you think it through.

The next time you have electronic or technological problems and it seems a bit out of the ordinary, ask yourself if there's a message here.

14. Weather

Most people who live in the same area will experience the same type of weather, so this might not seem like a message from the Universe. However, it's not the actual weather, but what you notice about it that's important. It could be raining outside and you don't pay much attention to it when suddenly you hear a crack of thunder, hail hits your window, the wind knocks down a tree branch, or the rain picks up in intensity. Anything that snaps you out of what you're doing and has you taking notice can be a sign.

It could be the Universe telling you to take a break and do something else. Maybe you need to focus on something more important or constructive. Perhaps you need to finally accomplish something you've been putting off.

I learned that last lesson the hard way. When we moved into our current house there was a small, dead tree close to the house. I kept thinking that with the next storm it could fall any time and break a window or worse. All I needed to do was call someone to cut the tree down and I'd have peace of mind. Unfortunately, I'm the type of person who often puts things off for another day. Well, my lesson came less than a month later.

We got a bad summer storm with high winds and that tree fell right on the back porch awning, damaging it. I was so grateful it didn't break the huge kitchen window. The very next day I called to have it removed. I thanked the Universe for giving me the kick in the butt I needed without the lesson being too expensive or catastrophic. I also made a promise to myself to take care of things right away rather than putting them off. Though I'm not perfect at it, I am doing better.

Storms can also tell you a lot about your current state of mind. For example, the storm we had and the tree falling? I was so happy that we recently moved but it was a big change, life was disrupted, and the energy in the house was less calm than I'm used to. Nothing was bad, the change was good, but we were combining two households and expecting my first grandbaby, so things were a bit in turmoil which matched my mood during that storm. Again, it wasn't bad, just very "chaotic".

15. Unusual or New Words

You've been alive for many years, heard countless words, but suddenly you hear or see a word you never had before. Maybe you start seeing this word again and again. Sometimes the Universe has trouble getting through to us in gentler ways and so it sends a word that will stop you and make you take notice.

This happened to me with the word "hyperbole". It was an editor from a publishing house I was with at the time who said I used hyperbole in some parts of my book. Well, I consider myself a well-rounded person when it comes to writing and the English language in general, but at the time it wasn't a word I'd ever encountered. (That might seem strange, but true.) I looked it up and read that it was an "extravagant exaggeration". Well, I was never so offended in all my life to read that! Okay, that was hyperbole. I got it. I did tend to go over the top in my books at times.

In less than a week I heard that word three more times. So I went from never hearing it to hearing it multiple times. I knew the Universe was trying to tell me something and, although it was unflattering, that it was about myself. I did tend to make the proverbial mountains out of molehills and be a bit dramatic at times. The message cut sort of deep, but I really took it to heart and made personal changes.

When I start hearing that word again, more than once, of course, I know I need to take a look at myself and see if I've been too dramatic or over the top about something recently. Sure enough, I always find it and I'm humbled once again.

The next time you come across a word you don't know the meaning to, or hear a word you haven't heard spoken in a very long time, you might want to pay attention to it.

16. Smells

Have you ever noticed how certain smells can propel you back to a time and place in the past? Sometimes you aren't even aware that your mind has made this connection until you encounter the smell again and this unexpected scent conjures powerful memories.

I have dozens of stories about how a smell has triggered a memory and taught me a lesson or reminded me of something important. The first one that comes to mind right now is when I worked for an inventory service. The pay was really good, but the hours were awful and the work was mind-numbing. However, I always believed that any job was better than no job at all.

One time we were all at a higher-end department store well before dawn to get the inventory done before opening. I was counting jewelry and nearby was the perfume counter. I was working, and feeling particularly hungry and stressed, when out of nowhere I got the strong scent of Lady Stetson. My grandmother wore that for many years. (Before that it was Tabu.) I knew they wouldn't sell that perfume at this store since it wasn't an expensive brand. Also, aside from the workers counting items, nobody else was there.

I knew it was my grandmother trying to get my attention. (And, yes, deceased loved ones are part of the Universe as well. Everything and everyone is.) At that moment I looked down at the enormous amounts of rings and other pieces of jewelry I needed to get through and admitted that this job was killing me. I was miserable, overworked, tired, and it just wasn't worth it. After finishing my shift I put in my two-week notice and never looked back. Days later I got serious about doing readings for clients. To this day I remember that as the worst job I had and was so grateful that my grandmother and the Universe intervened.

A friend of mine smells baking bread when she hasn't spent enough time with her family. When she was younger her mother made bread every Sunday. It was her way of showing her love and bringing the family together for a special meal. A client of mine smells lavender whenever the Universe tells her she needs to pamper herself more, and another one smells cedar wood when she needs to take a break and spend more time in nature.

The next time you smell something familiar that seems to come out of nowhere, ask yourself what this scent triggers and what message it might have for you.

17. Memory Triggers

The day seems pretty normal then suddenly something or someone sparks a memory in you, whether good or bad. You see or smell something that reminds you of a friend you haven't talked to in a while. This can be a sign from the Universe that it's time for a reunion either in person or just through phone or email. Something inside you needs this connection at this point in time. Or, you see someone who reminds you of a person who hurt you in the past and this can signal that you have unfinished emotional issues to process before you can fully move on.

You could also get a memory trigger about a loved one who's crossed over. Maybe you need to reconnect with them by just mentally letting them know they're still in your heart, or you could have a small memorial in their honor or visit their grave.

When I was a young teenager a next-door neighbor was a sweet lady who grew lots and lots of plants. She made my sister a Halloween costume and sometimes brought a casserole to our house so our working mom wouldn't have to cook. I have really fond memories of her.

One day I was going for a checkup at the doctor and noticed a jade plant in a big pot near the front door. It sparked a memory of this neighbor and how she had several of these plants in her backyard. I smiled, looked heavenward, and right after my appointment, went to the nursery and bought a jade plant in her honor. I think of her every time I see it on my windowsill. Anything that will commemorate a loved one who has passed on is wonderful and keeps them alive in spirit.

18. Obstacles

An obstacle on your path could come in the form of a setback, a delay, a detour, a roadblock, an injury, or an illness. They also seem to come out of nowhere. You're on your way to an important interview and you get a flat tire. You're all set to go on a vacation and you come down with the flu and can't go. You saved up to buy something you thought you really wanted then need to use that money for an unexpected car repair, home repair, or vet bill.

These obstacles can be frustrating but very often it's the Universe stepping in to get us going in another direction or making us wait until the time is right. These things are always something out of your control and the best you can do is take a step back and view it as a sign.

19. Destruction

Everything is going wrong or falling apart. You can't imagine things getting worse, yet it does. Life is filled with one catastrophe or hardship after another, or the frustrations and annoyances pile up with no end in sight. It's times like these when we feel the most alone and abandoned. There can't possibly be any great Universal energy, no spirit guides or angels or even God if they let these things happen! This is just the ego lashing out at the seeming unfairness of it all.

I'm not talking about people getting cancer or a loved one passing away because grief is on a whole different level. But when it comes to everyday things mounting and burying you under the rubble, consider this as an invitation to change and an opportunity to awaken. Nothing gets our attention more than everything going wrong all at once.

Very often, it's the Universe getting us to reevaluate how we've been living our lives. When life is stable and things don't change we become complacent and stop learning and growing. Hardships force you to rethink things and start over again in ways that ultimately align with who you truly are.

20. During Meditation

Although I don't meditate as much as I used to, when I do it's like opening the door for the Universe to send through signs, guidance, and answers. When you meditate you go deep within yourself, away from the problems and distractions of the outside world, and this is where vast amounts of knowledge and wisdom start flowing.

Before you meditate you can ask a question you need an answer to or something you want guidance on. See what information comes through as you relax your mind and are one with the Universe. So often the answers were inside us all along.

21. Everything Is Smooth

Your life is flowing along, things are lining up perfectly, you feel inspired, positive, and opportunities are abundant. You're accomplishing your goals and your dreams are becoming reality.

In these times you're in alignment with the Universe and living as your authentic self. This is who you're meant to be, how you're meant to feel, and you're on the right path!

Being in this zone might last months, weeks, or mere hours, but when you're in it life feels amazing. One of the nice things about being in this state of alignment is that, even if it doesn't last long, once you've had a taste of it you can recapture it again and again. And, very often, it will last longer each time it comes around. When it does, make the most of it and run with this wonderful energy. Accomplish as much as possible and reap the rewards.

As you see, the Universe can communicate with you in so many ways. When you get more used to recognizing this help you'll find what works best for you. Some people get most of their guidance in dreams while others rely on signs that repeat themselves. Over time you'll discover how you and the Universe work together best. One thing to keep in mind, no matter how this communication comes through, is that anything that repeats is proof positive that the Universe is trying to tell you something.

When you do receive signs, try not to overthink things. I've done this far too many times and it just made me more anxious and confused when that's the exact opposite of what the Universe wants for us. The messages we get truly are simple, but as humans we often overanalyze. Our logic and egos get in the way and block the way. Trust the Universe and trust your intuition. If something doesn't make complete sense right now or you can't figure out what you're being told, rest assured that it will all come together very soon.

Warning Signs

Most of the signs the Universe sends will be gentler, meant to get your attention so you can figure things out for yourself. There are times though when it steps in with bigger wake-up calls, hoping you truly take notice and take the advice.

1. Last-Minute Delays

Something happens and you can't make it to your destination. You get stuck in traffic, your plane is delayed or the flight you need is completely booked, an important interview with a potential new employer gets canceled, your school loan fell through, or you didn't get that house you wanted.

These delays or cancellations come out of nowhere and throw off your plans, perhaps even your goals or dreams. It's easy to be upset, I know I have been, but then I take a step back and ask myself, "If this seemed like such a sure thing or so simple or so great why did it get messed up like this?"

Since I'm a firm believer in most things happening for a reason, I look more deeply and admit that perhaps it wasn't for my highest good, my ultimate happiness, or just wasn't the right place or the right time.

If it's meant to be, the opportunity will come around again, or something better will instead.

2. Gut Feelings

Whether we're talking about a person, a place, or a thing, if you get a sinking feeling in the pit of your stomach or your intuition is loudly telling you something just isn't right, you *need* to pay attention.

It's far too easy to ignore our own feelings and many times this can result in something as small as frustration to something much bigger. Let me give you a few examples of this. Years ago, I met my son-in-law's new friend. Nothing seemed off, he was polite and laughed a lot, but for some reason, my stomach churned whenever I was around him. He had lots of friends, he was popular, but no matter what, if he was at a get-together and I was there too I would avoid him. If he came over to talk to me I felt nauseated and I'd make an excuse to go do something just to get away from him. Eventually, it came out that he was a pedophile and is now serving time in prison.

Another time I was taking a plane to see my oldest daughters who were living in Maryland and I had a connecting flight. For some reason I got a very uneasy feeling about this and, because my mind tends to think the worst, I wondered if the plane was going to crash. The time between the connecting flights was tight yet I took my time walking to the next gate and missed getting on that plane. I ended up taking a later flight and got to my destination safe and sound.

I looked into what happened with my original flight and there was a mechanical problem that had the plane stuck on the tarmac for more than four hours. Eventually, it got so late everyone had to sleep at the airport until the next available flight.

Thankfully, it was nothing deadly, but it was definitely an inconvenience and one I avoided by listening to my intuition.

3. Misplacing or Losing Items

Have you ever found that for some reason you keep losing or misplacing something? It might be the same item or different ones, but this is a sign from the Universe telling you to pay attention. It's so easy for us to be distracted and forget where we put something while our minds are somewhere else. The next time this happens, and if it's recurring, ask yourself what the connection is.

My daughter kept misplacing her work badge and each time had to pay $30 to have it replaced. This happened at least every other month. Finally, I asked her why she was subconsciously doing this and she seemed taken aback. She assured me it was accidental but when I pressed her she admitted she didn't like her job. Eventually, she talked to her supervisor and was honest about her feelings. Rather than being let go as she feared, they found another department for her and she's much happier—and hasn't lost her work badge since!

This next example might sound sad, but one of my clients kept misplacing her engagement ring. It seemed to fit fine, but she'd wash her hands and it would fall off, she'd take it off while she was working in the garden and somehow misplaced it, and so on. Saying that she lost that ring a dozen times within three years is an understatement.

We had talked about this subject before, but I brought it up again. After all, she wanted a relationship reading and I was being paid to be honest and offer guidance. I asked her how she really felt about their relationship and upcoming wedding and she finally admitted that she was incredibly unsure. Although her fiance was ready, willing, and able to settle down and move in together, she enjoyed her freedom and wanted to focus on her career. I told her that it was unfair to them both to keep dragging this out and she needed to be honest with him. The problem was, she didn't want to be alone either.

Eventually, she told him how she felt and, although he was disappointed and hurt, he understood. He wanted someone ready for marriage and he broke off the engagement, but you know what? My client is actually doing great as a single lady and knows when the time is right the right guy will come along. And her ex? He found someone else very soon and was married less than six months later.

4. Insomnia

Whether you have trouble falling asleep or wake up in the middle of the night and can't fall back to sleep, insomnia is often a sign that you need to pay attention to something. Focus on your thoughts and ask yourself if you're feeling worried, afraid, angry, or uncertain. Sometimes you'll know exactly what's on your mind and these constant thoughts and feelings mean you need to take care of it, get through it, or let it go.

Other times you won't know why you have these runaway thoughts that bounce from one thing to the next. When this happens, look at the common theme of your thoughts or the feeling that ties them all together. Even if there seems to be no connection, if you're having trouble sleeping and your thoughts are going in circles, there's a reason for it.

In my own life, when I have insomnia and notice all these awful things from my past popping up, or things in the future that haven't happened and most likely won't, I know I'm stressed about something. My mind has a frustrating way of hiding what the reason is though. None of the thoughts or memories seem connected, but I know the Universe is trying to get me to take notice and take care of something. So, I'll start going over things happening in my life in the here and now, what events could have triggered this, and I always discover the stressor.

5. Injury or Illnesses

If you find that you keep getting sick, develop headaches, strain a muscle, or anything else that prevents you from doing something, don't ignore it. This could be a message for you to slow down and take better care of yourself. Or, you might not want to do something and this is your subconscious way of getting out of it.

A while back, a woman came to me for a reading on why she would get a chronic migraine, like clockwork, on the same day of the week. We talked about her lifestyle, diet, and other things, but then I said, "What do you need to do but don't want to do every Monday?" After thinking about it, she said it was the first day of the workweek and she didn't like her supervisor.

Although she didn't have to see him often, every Monday morning there would be a meeting that went on for too long. He would talk nonstop, point out everyone's faults, and wore cologne that was far too strong. I mentioned that her migraines could be triggered by stress, but also the smell of his cologne.

Sure enough, she went to see her doctor and this is exactly what it was. Her job paid well and she liked it, and there was no way she could get out of the Monday meetings, but just knowing where these migraines were coming from and why helped her to get through them.

Another client developed a knee problem when she was much younger because she didn't like playing soccer. Her father was hoping she'd get a scholarship and was proud to tell everyone about his soccer-playing daughter. She didn't have the heart to tell him she had other plans for her future so subconsciously developed this knee problem that had her removed from the team. Once she discovered why she had this chronic pain, even more than a decade later, she talked to her father about it. Very soon, the pain vanished and she has full mobility again.

6. Negative Signs

What one person might consider a negative sign might mean the exact opposite to someone else. When you encounter something that seems negative for you, think about what it could be pointing to.

One summer, a friend of mine wanted me to go on a trip with her. At the time I couldn't afford it but I didn't want to disappoint her. I hadn't given her an answer yet, but the signs I got just in one single day had me being honest with her.

On the way to the store, there was a brand new stop sign at an intersection that hadn't been there before. A few more streets down there was a stoplight that was out so I had to proceed with caution. While in the parking lot looking for a space to park a cart came out of nowhere and I had to slam on the brakes so I wouldn't hit it.

All of these things registered with me, saying, "Stop what you're doing!" My friend was disappointed but understood and found someone else to go with her. They both had a great time but ended up with food poisoning that ruined the last three days of the trip. I was extra glad I hadn't gone!

7. Recurring Obstacles

No matter how hard you try or how much you do, you can't reach your goal. One thing after another gets in your way, preventing you from getting somewhere or getting something done. When this happens I know the Universe is trying to get my attention. I take a moment to think about how I've been going about something and make changes (since I was obviously getting nowhere doing what I was before) or letting it go completely if it isn't anything hugely important.

Most people don't do this though. We dig in our heels and try even harder, and keep doing the same things that haven't been working. Instead of wasting valuable time and effort, the next time you keep encountering roadblocks, take it as a sign to do something different.

When You Receive Warnings

Everyone will get sick or injured at some point, have insomnia occasionally, or run across any of the above signs we just talked about. If you sprain your ankle it doesn't necessarily mean the Universe is telling you you're on the wrong path. If you get anxious before a date it doesn't always mean that this person isn't the one for you. It's far too easy to become consumed with what we think the Universe might be saying until it becomes a crippling obsession that has you frozen in place.

Usually, signs will be repeated or a whole lot happens at once so you can be sure it's the Universe sending a message and not just everyday life happenings. Also, you're not being punished, it's just a sign to pay attention. Ask yourself what you're doing, thinking, pursuing, or planning right now that might not be for your highest good. Where are you compromising yourself? Where are you not living as your authentic self? Where are you covering up? What are you putting up with? What needs to change or become more stable?

The signs will usually be a whisper at first, but if you don't pay attention and figure things out the Universe will get louder and the signs will become bigger until you finally get it. When you do receive signs, try to be proactive rather than worrying or stressing yourself out. Too often I've gotten tense, bracing myself for something negative to happen, when in reality the message was just to pay attention, make a change, or take action.

Finding Your Soulmate

―――

I've included this section because I get so many requests for relationship readings. People want to know if they're going to eventually be with a soulmate, if someone they're with now is a soulmate, if a past partner was their one true love and they lost that chance, or when and where they'll meet "the one".

If you've gone on many dates but you didn't click with anyone, have been in too many short-term relationships, or were left brokenhearted after a long-term relationship it's easy to think you'll never find that special someone.

Sometimes it feels easier to give up altogether or just settle for anyone at all just so you don't have to be alone. Being alone for the right reasons is healthy, but being with someone for the wrong reasons will just make you miserable.

When you're feeling lonely or your relationship is going down the drain it's because you've ignored your own feelings, your intuition, and the signs from the Universe. We are *always* being guided to our best possible life, as long as we pay attention and take action. The problem with humans is we get lazy and become deaf and blind to the signs that can show us how to be happier, healthier, more successful, and deeply in love. A good life takes work and too many people just give up.

Maybe you believe you've been open to signs but nothing has come your way. Does that mean the Universe isn't trying to help you? Does it mean you should throw in the towel where love is concerned? Not at all. There's someone for everyone and if you want to be in love, know that you deserve it. Best of all, the Universe can send you signs letting you know that a relationship is coming into your life very soon.

While it's true that some signs from the Universe are loud and clear, most of the time they're quieter and easy to miss. If you pay close attention though you'll be able to detect these signs that will guide you to a positive relationship.

So far, we've talked about all the ways the Universe can communicate with you such as coincidences, dreams, song lyrics, or setbacks. Even random strangers can bring important messages and guidance. Can the Universe really help you find your soulmate though? That seems like a big order to fill, though nothing is too big for the Universe. Some things that get in the way of people finding true love are:

- Not paying attention to the signs.

- Not taking time to heal.

- Feeling they aren't worthy of true love.

- Expecting absolute perfection from a person or relationship.

- Still in a relationship while trying to find another.

- Mentally, physically, or emotionally not ready for love.

A soulmate union is something almost everyone hopes to find in life, yet very few ever do. This type of love means you're with a person who can make you feel special, happy, excited, and comfortable. You can be yourself and they can be themselves. It's a sense of connection, even if you don't share the same interests, because you're connected at a much deeper level than just likes and dislikes.

That all sounds wonderful, right? So how do you learn to be open to the clues and signs that will alert you to this special person? Actually, soulmate signs from the Universe are easy to detect, and acting on them will eventually lead you to the type of love you've always wanted.

As you'll see, most of these "signs" are inside of you, not outside. Why is this though? After all, we've been talking about seeing and hearing things out in the world that can point us in the right direction or get us to take notice, so why are signs from the Universe about love different? Because, you can't find true love and enjoy a long-term soulmate union if you aren't mentally and emotionally ready. You'll simply keep attracting what you already have been for so long. Here are some signs that point to love being on the near horizon for you.

1. You've Let Go Of The Past

When you think of an ex you don't feel hurt or angry anymore. Your mind doesn't rehash old arguments or things that person did that made you angry or made you cry. You know that nobody is perfect, you both made mistakes, but you no longer blame them or yourself for the breakup. This is one of the biggest signs that you're ready for love and that your soulmate is just around the corner.

2. You Gave Yourself Time To Heal

Far too often, people get into a new relationship right after getting out of one, or even before the breakup. They don't allow themselves time to heal or process anything and this results in a rebound relationship that usually doesn't last long because you're dragging all your baggage along with you.

Taking time out after a split will allow you to work through things and enter into a new relationship as a whole person. We can always learn something from the people we've been with, so take your past relationships and use them as lessons that will get you closer to finding your soulmate.

3. You Stop Wasting Time

You're completely done with people who don't appreciate you and make you second-guess whether they care about you or not. You're no longer interested in jumping right into things then seeing where it all goes. You know that when the right person comes your way there will be no doubt about how they feel because they'll show you and tell you.

And, now that you've healed from your past relationships, you'll quickly dump anyone who isn't worthy of your love. You'll no longer waste time and energy on someone who isn't right for you. You know your worth and this confidence attracts someone who will give you the love and respect you deserve.

4. You're Happy To See Other Happy Couples

Rather than feeling sad or annoyed when you see other couples in love, it makes you happy for them and hopeful for your own love life. Once you notice that you're seeing more and more couples who seem blissfully in love, it's a sure sign that love is coming your way. You can't see in the world what doesn't exist within yourself. We see what we project outwards. If you're seeing love it's because you're on that same vibrational plane, and this will attract your soulmate.

5. Having Romantic Dreams

When you're feeling hurt and angry over a breakup—whether it was a week ago or a decade ago—you're probably not going to have dreams about finding love. When you do notice that your dreams are changing and there's love, romance, or sex involved it shows that you're healing. You might dream of complete strangers, famous people, or even an ex.

The Universe is simply letting you know that you're in the right frame of mind for finding love. Since your subconscious is changing it means that your energy field is changing and will soon attract true love.

6. Coincidences and Synchronicities

If you keep seeing a certain symbol, especially one that relates to love such as a heart, engagement rings, wedding ads, the word "love", or things of this nature it could be a sign from the Universe that love will be coming into your life very soon. It's preparing you mentally and energetically for a new relationship so be sure to pay attention to these signs.

You could also see repeating numbers, letting you know that your life will be changing in some way very soon.

Or, you could even hear from one or more exes. This shows that you're ready for a new relationship and your energy is so strong that your ex is thinking about you. Some people take this as a sign to get back with their ex, though this is rarely the message here. You broke up for a reason and it's extremely rare when giving an old relationship another try will work out. Instead, use your relationships of the past as lessons to make you a better person and to know what you desire and deserve in a soulmate union.

7. You're More Positive

Rather than wasting time thinking about negative things and spending time with negative people you focus on the positive. You don't want toxic energy flowing in your life and find it easy to let go of anything and anyone that's poison to your pursuit of happiness. You focus on your goals and your mental, physical, emotional, and spiritual health.

Releasing negativity is important for life in general, but especially important in attracting true love. You want to radiate the most positive energy you can and know that your unspoken message will be heard and attract that special person.

8. You Feel Happy

You'll know you're in the right mindset for love and you've done a lot of internal healing when you're perfectly happy being alone. You aren't in a relationship and yet you feel patient and relaxed. There's no sense of urgency or desperation to find another partner. You're content with being single and know that when the time is right love will arrive. When you're in this zone you're spreading positive energy that will attract your soulmate.

A happy, stable relationship can't find you if you haven't done any work on yourself. You'll simply keep attracting what you have before because like attracts like. Whoever you've been with in the past was attracted to your energy field at the time.

When you feel complete as a single person you won't be looking for someone to *make* you happy since you're happy on your own. You find this happiness by focusing on yourself first and foremost. The moment you no longer need a significant other is usually when they arrive.

Receiving and Interpreting Signs

It's easy to be skeptical that we can receive helpful signs and guidance from the Universe. It can't be proven by science so it's easy to stick it in the realm of fantasy. Instead, we're taught to follow logic over feelings, and follow the crowd instead of our personal wants, needs, and desires. Of course, people are allowed to believe what they want to, but why close yourself off to free 24/7 help and guidance?

By having a genuine desire to open yourself up to what the Universe wants to tell you, by becoming curious and eager for its signs, you can make your life bigger, better, and happier than it's ever been. Not only that, but you can learn to avoid many of the things in life that have held you back or knocked you off course.

Once you start living in alignment with your true self the Universe will help you even more. And, the more comfortable you become with following this advice, the more successful you'll be in all areas of life. How do you start receiving and interpreting all these signs though?

1. Become More Receptive

One of the best ways to increase your receptivity is to read books just like this one. It helps to open you up so you're more aware of how the signs from the Universe can help you and how to spot them and interpret them. When you start acting on these signs and seeing how they positively impact your life it opens you up to even more signs and all the positive help that can come your way.

Signs can be very literal, such as a TV commercial or billboard telling you to do something specific—like with my long-overdue eye exam. Others though take time to interpret or are more subtle. Even so, these will eventually make sense, even if it's in hindsight. Still others are unique to each person such as a smell, color, object, or another symbol that pertains to your personal life somehow whether past or present.

2. Look Outward

We all need to look inward a whole lot more than we usually do, whether we're analyzing ourselves, doing visualization, affirmations, or meditation. We also need to look outward just as much so we can see what the Universe and world around us are trying to teach us.

You don't have to have to hyper-focus on everything all the time but by being alert to what you see when you're out, when you're at work, or even at home, you'll start to see more things that are worth taking note of.

When you're first starting out, you'll naturally be more aware than usual. It's perfectly fine to notice five or more things every day that could potentially be signs from the Universe. Over time you'll get much better at weeding out the important from the mundane. Even if what you think is a sign for you turns out to be nothing, just being open to it increases your ability to spot more relevant signs when they do pop up.

3. Look For Patterns

The first step to recognizing signs from the Universe is picking them out. That is, anything that seems unusual, interesting, or calls your attention in some way. Once you've gotten used to this, the next step is to increase your ability to spot patterns and recurring experiences or events. Whether you write these down or simply remember them, the key is to make this a normal part of your day until it's second nature.

The way the Universe works is it will typically send you repeating signs/patterns that lead you to what you need to do next in life. That doesn't mean that you have no say over your destiny and that you're just being led around like a pet on a leash. Instead, you're given these clues that can help you discover your own purpose, find happiness, and offer you comfort.

Last week my youngest daughter kept encountering "The Terminator". Three times in one day something came up about this movie. A show on TV mentioned it, she saw the poster while out somewhere, a random person was overheard saying "I'll be back" which was the famous line from Arnold Schwarzenegger in one of The Terminator movies. Since I raised my girls to pay attention to signs, as well as their intuition, she knew this was important.

When she went to work a few days later her boss was in a terrible mood because her fiance broke up with her. Needless to say, she was emotionally devastated, but instead of talking about it to a friend or relative, she decided to fire her whole department. My daughter was pretty sick of this woman's attitude in general since she tended to take her emotions out on her employees so she gladly packed her stuff and left, though she did love the job itself.

Well, wouldn't you know it, less than 24 hours later she called everyone to apologize, tell them what happened, and hired them all back—with a pay raise. So, she was terminated (The Terminator) but she was rehired (I'll be back).

If she hadn't spotted these patterns she would have been caught off guard and upset, but seeing the signs beforehand helped her to stay calm, and she knew that it would all be okay in the end.

4. Taking Chances

Let's say you're looking for love again and come across an advertisement for a new restaurant or a band you like that's touring and will be in your town. It's far easier to meet someone when you're out and about rather than being at home all the time, right? So why not try that restaurant or invite a friend to see that band?

You very well could meet your soulmate there, or meet someone who will eventually introduce you to them. If nothing else, you're getting out and having a good time which increases the positive energy of your aura, which in turn attracts more positive people and opportunities. It's a win-win situation either way.

5. Go With The Flow

It's easy to get into all of these signs, see signs everywhere, try to interpret them, and think that everything is important—either as a happy opportunity or negative warning. This is completely normal and I sometimes still get caught up in this myself.

We often see what we want to see or what we fear most. It's a sign that this person is a soulmate! It's a sign that I'll win the lottery! It's a sign that I'll get into an accident or get a horrible illness! This isn't how the Universe works. Even if something seems negative, know in your heart that whatever happens is going to lead you to something better—like my daughter with The Terminator clues. It seemed negative but ended up being positive in the end.

The Universe isn't trying to make you afraid of the future, punish you, or dictate every step you take. It wants to help you become the best person you can be, living your best life. All signs are meant to help you grow and lead you to your true potential.

If you're looking for an answer or some guidance, simply ask for it. When you encounter a sign, view yourself as a passive recipient of that information, and consciously let go of how you think things will play out or how you want them to. Allow everything to unfold naturally.

Trust that the Universe really does know what's best for you, even if what it wants to show you or guide you to isn't what you expected. Not all gifts come wrapped the way we expect them to.

Connecting With The Universe

The Universe will always help guide you down the best paths in life if you learn to tune in and listen. Let's say you've been getting signs lately but you aren't sure what to do with them. Here are some ways to connect with the Universe so you're both on the same wavelength.

- Am I On The Right Path?

To find out whether or not you're currently on the right path you'll need to tune into your intuition. It's not easy at first, but with practice, you'll get much better at it. Think about something you're currently pursuing and ask the question either out loud or in your mind, "Am I on the right path?"

Now, pay attention to any sensations in your body. As you scan yourself from head to toe notice if any areas feel tense, heavy, or painful. If so, this could be a sign that you need to change something. Or, do you feel light, happy, and warm? This is most likely a sign that you're on the right path and no changes are needed at the moment.

- Asking For Guidance

Every morning before I start my day I say a short affirmation so I'm open to any messages the Universe wants to send me. I sit on my bed, take a few deep breaths, and mentally say, "Universe, thank you for your guidance today. Please help me to be awake and aware of what I need to change or do for my highest good, and alert me when I'm on the wrong path."

Sometimes I'll end things there or, if it feels right, I spend some time in introspection, being receptive to anything that might come through. If I receive anything I'll make a note of it in my journal. I also write down notes at the end of the day on any signs or guidance I encountered. Writing things down helps me to be more focused and open to the guidance of the Universe.

If you don't receive signs right away, know that you will when the time is right. The Universe moves when we're meant to move, not when *we* believe we should. Everything needs to line up a certain way so your path is clear and as smooth as possible. If the road is rocky it's a sure sign it's time to make some changes. Ask for guidance and wait to see what information comes your way.

The Universe Has Your Back

———

You never need to feel alone or that you'll never know what to do or how to do something. The Universe is always here to guide you and give you answers. You're always supported and any confusion, fear, or obstacles will be removed once you get out of your own way.

More often than not we create our own obstacles, and this is because we always want control. It makes us feel safer, though boxes us in or makes a mess of things. Simply keep your eyes and ears open for the signs, trust that you're being guided and supported, and take advantage of any opportunities that come your way.

And you know what? It's completely up to you what you decide to do with the signs the Universe sends you. Sometimes you might be completely open and ready to follow the new path before you. Other times you might not want to deal with it.

When the Universe talks to me I don't always listen. Maybe I'm tired, overworked, or perhaps life is going along well and I just don't want to disrupt the current road I'm on. *That's okay.* It will come around again with other opportunities and guidance. The Universe will never abandon you and will send more signs when you're ready.

One thing I've learned though is that when you pay attention and notice these signs your perspective eventually changes. You see things in new ways that you wouldn't have before and without a second thought, your soul embraces this new direction and follows it.

Contact Me/Book A Reading

Whether your problems or concerns are in the areas of love, finances, family, career, health, education, or your path in life, I offer professional intuitive counseling, caring guidance, and solutions that work!

I use no tools. Instead, I'll connect directly with your higher self and your spirit guides to help you through any situation and achieve the best possible results. No problem is too big or too small, and your questions will be answered in detail.

I'll let you know absolutely everything that comes through in the reading which typically includes past, present, and future energies, guidance, time frames and predictions. Each reading is in-depth, filled with positive energy and guidance, and includes one free clarification email.

All readings are done via email. By offering my readings through email you'll be able to save your reading and go back to it again and again for guidance.

I look forward to reading for you!

Check out my readings, books, blog posts, and more on my website:

D[1]rKellyPsychic.com

Or email me directly at: DrKellyPsychicCounselor@gmail.com

Printed in Great Britain
by Amazon

32727215R00047